For Our Children

Family Unity & The Old Ways

Writing Template

Written By

Peter Laidlaw

Table of Contents

Family Template

It is not my intention for everyone to believe everything in this book is geared for them. One purpose of this book is for use as a template for families to write their own stories. To summarize their ways of living and pass them on to future generations. The subject matters can be used as guidelines to write words of wisdom from your own people and their perspectives. This is an opportunity to pool members of your family of all ages to assist those coming after they are gone. So much wisdom and experience to share in one book or place.

One dream that I envisioned is this information can be kept for your own families or shared with others so people of different races and creeds can learn from it. Wouldn't it be great if families could post their own beliefs on a worldwide database for others to gain wisdom and understanding from? I am willing to believe that we are not that different as races and the way we think. Understanding each other is the first step in working together as humans. Not quite sure if people would feel comfortable doing that but it is a possibility.

The book is broken up into different sections. Use those sections to insert your own family beliefs and stories or add to the ones that my family uses. Either way it is a good start. My family passed along a lot of wisdom but never wrote it down. This is your chance to do it for your family by following my template as a guideline. Good luck!

Template Format

Family Template – use this format to create your own family book to pass on to future generations.

Summary – what are you trying to create.

Introduction – what are you trying to say.

Letters to our children – what would you say to your children about the family's future.

Why write this book – the importance of writing it.

Your ancestors – what people make up your family.

Our family dynamics concerns – what we could become.

Our society – how society acts sometimes. Your definition.

Family code – how to conduct your behavior.

Kids advice – how the children should behave.

Our way of life – how we live.

Our system – how we act.

The old ways of thinking – what is important.

Old ways words to live by – key words to contemplate and understand.

The old ways philosophies – key philosophies to understand.

My terms – how can I change as I get older and wiser.

What I believe in – what is important to me.

Things I don't like – what turns me off.

Great books I have read – wisdom library

Preparing for the future – building your life for future success.

Who was he – what did I do to improve and build my life.

Forgive yourself – accept your mistakes and move on in life.

What I am grateful for – list them

Dear God – what do you want from God.

Summary

It is important to explain why a particular book has been written. Most books are written for a purpose and to get a specific point or points across to the reader. This book is written to motivate others to action. To give all of you a purpose and meaning to your life. To create unity in your life that you never had before. It will not be easy and nothing you do to create change in your life is.

My name is Peter Matthew Laidlaw and it is the year 2024. Our society has changed drastically since I was a boy. Most historians will point out that this is normal. In most cases, I would agree with them but not now. We have become a society of confused and misunderstood humans where a lot of people want to make excuses for their actions rather than take responsibility for them. Our government has become more broken than any other time in our history. Gas prices are soaring as well as the price of just about every product we buy. Most families are struggling to survive. Men, women, and children have become brain washed by all the social media and television messages bombarding them every day. So what do we do about it? Everybody has the capacity to change if they are willing.

Have you ever taken the time to think of what it would be like to have a life of purpose? To live and work in an environment that you actually enjoyed and got along with the people there. That is what I am searching for. Not just the same old existence. We can get there but it begins with unity.

We have to set aside our differences between race, color and creed to become one working unit. We have two arms, two legs, ten fingers and toes, one head two ears, one mouth, etc. The only thing that is different amongst us as human beings is the way we think, the color of our eyes and skin. We can make this happen, but it will require change by everyone. We have to stop making excuses and take responsibility for our actions. If you make a mistake, then there are consequences. These are the key building blocks to "THE OLD WAYS". The easiest way for me to show you this system is to use my family as an example. This book is not a platform to brag about my family. It is used to show others what can be accomplished with effort, discipline and dedication in your life.

This book is separated into two distinct areas. The first area is our philosophy for running a family unit. The second area is guidelines for different subjects of how to cope in certain situations. Many of you may have recommendations on improving these guidelines which is fantastic. I challenge you to create a book that is similar to this one for your own family. The key to getting us back to the society we once were begins with creating UNITY. We need to create a CLAN mentality to bring all of these units together. We need to create a system for our children and grandchildren that will protect us and open up more opportunity for success. If you have an interest in changing your life and that of others, then turn the page and let us begin.

Loyalty

To defend one's family and friends by whatever means necessary to protect and honor them. If you gain a person's trust and respect, there is a great chance you will achieve their loyalty. Loyalty can't be bought and has to be earned. It is the easiest to lose and the hardest to ever get back. It should never be taken lightly.

Laidlaw Rule

We may never be rich, but what we share together as a family unit has far more value than money alone.

Peter Matthew Laidlaw

Introduction

Dear Children,

I am writing this book for you for one reason: To help guide you through life after I am gone. It is filled with past and present generations of Laidlaw's examples, plans, experiences, stories and wisdom. For many years, my parents and grandparents passed on great wisdom and knowledge of their experiences. Unfortunately, they never wrote anything down or recorded their hopes, dreams, failures or successes. This is my attempt to do so to honor them and help you through tough times.

There are many examples of when a parent has died and their children have crumbled or done things out of character to hurt themselves. That is not the wishes of me or your ancestors. You must carry on as generations before you have and be the best that you can be. You must give our family name the proper respect it deserves and tarnish it in no way. You are the hope and dreams of the future for our family.

I have given all of you some direction on how to behave and conduct yourself while on earth at one time or another. You are all beautiful and talented in your own way.

Go out there and show the world your power and make me proud!

I Love You!

Always and Forever!

Dad

Letters To Our Children

Family Unity – Message 1

Dear Children,

I originally set out to write a book that I thought could change the mindset of the people of this world. Instead, I've decided to write a book for families to possibly do that. The world is a strange place. Human beings can be so kind and yet cruel toward each other. This book is written to prepare you in how to deal with this world.

I do not consider myself an expert in all things. Only a fool would believe that. However, I have experienced a lot of situations first hand and learned many things from a lot of good people. Those are the issues I will discuss and hope to guide you with. No, I don't have a doctorate in human behavior. I did go to the school of "hard knocks" and have learned from a lot of stupid mistakes I don't want you to repeat.

Should you feel a need to share or discuss some of our ideas with others, I'm okay with that. Just know that I felt it important enough to put my thoughts and wisdom learned in a book for my family. It's not meant for profit, ego or anything else other than I truly love all of you and hope that you are happy and successful in your lives.

Love ya,

Dad

Message 2

One of my biggest concerns is leaving this earth without passing on some of the wisdom and experiences that we have shared with each other over the years. That is why I would like to define this book as a living document.

I would like to ask all of my children and additional family members to contribute information on various subjects toward the improvement and preservation of this family for generations to come.

Each year or when you want to re-publish the book, do so to pass on to others. I know of no other book like this one that I can find at this time. I would also like to encourage others to use it as a template of their own. Families can create one themselves based on their families' teachings.

Why Write This Book?

Eliminate in-fighting within the family. A guide for future generations to reference in times of trouble or doubt. It is written for them.

There are two main reasons why this book is being written. The first is for you, the reader. There are many generations that have come before you and, God-willing, others that will come after you. There have been many lessons, experiences and guidelines passed on from our ancestors that to my knowledge have never been documented. This is rather sad because my parents shared so many great stories and lessons with me and other family members throughout our entire lives.

Many of you, I will never meet personally for our lives on this earth only lasts but a short period of time. I did want you to know however, that I thought enough of you as my own blood to write a reference guide to help and assist you in the future. Some of the things you read you will agree with and others you will not. Your uniqueness is what makes you a special part of this family and it is essential that you question and improve this book.

There are a lot of good ideas and concepts that you should be able to apply to your daily lives. They are presented before you to help and not set before you to try and tell you how to live your life specifically. Knowing this family, the way that I do, that is the last thing I want to do. We all have ideas on what the best way to live is. That is great. The main point is to throw out ideas that may help you. Use what you desire and pass it on.

The second reason for writing this book is to prevent in-fighting within the family. Within our own immediate family there have been many disagreements. With a large family, you are going to have circumstances that come up that test the integrity and patience of its members. Over the years, there have been times when we did not talk nor communicate with each other. Looking back at it now, it was such a waste of time. Myself, as an example, did not talk with my father for a year over a minor dispute. When he died, I realized that I missed one whole year of being with him. I tell you this because I beg you not to make the same mistake as me. Make every effort to remain united. Don't allow outsiders to cause friction within the family unit. If you have a disagreement, resolve it as quickly as you can.

Our society has changed a great deal. It is important to maintain a certain way of thinking so as not to get bogged down by all the inaccurate information we are getting on a daily basis. As a member of this family I am extremely proud of all of you. Hopefully, some of the concepts in this book will assist you in your lives. We owe it to each other and our ancestors to do the right thing and live exceptional lives. Best wishes to all of you.

Saving Our Families
Your Ancestors – Family Tree

Father and Mother – Al Laidlaw and Helen Doherty

Children – my parents had 7 children, 5 boys and 2 girls

Grandchildren – my parent's children had 15 children, 9 boys and 6 girls

Great grandchildren – my parent's children's children had 20 children, 12 boys and 8 girls

Grandparents – my parent's parents were of Scotch and Irish decent

Uncles and Aunts – my father had a brother and sister. My mother had one sister and brother.

Military Family – my family has been represented by all five services. Air Force, Marines, Army, Navy and Coast Guard. Some of our research has us fighting in the Civil War from Maine, WWI, WWII, Korean and Vietnam wars. There may be further data going back to the Revolutionary war but uncertain at this time. Many of my ancestors have received medals for heroism and being wounded in combat. My father used to say "the real heroes were the ones that never came back and sacrificed their lives for our freedom". He also said that war was "hell on earth" there was nothing glorious about it. Everything is destroyed and lives are sacrificed.

Success Stories – Professions

My father was an engineer who worked for Raytheon Corporation for 30 years. He was part of a group that helped launch the Apollo missions to the moon in the 1960's. My mother was offered a scholarship to college in high school to Tufts University but was made to go to work to support her family. It was rare for women to be offered any kind of scholarship in those days. My siblings, myself and our children have been successful in their careers. There are engineers, doctors, medical professionals, teachers, finance and accounting people, directors, supervisors, leaders in all disciplines. There are maintenance people, mechanics, cosmetologists, bar tenders, writers, and other various fields.

Sports, music, dance, cheer leading, acting are activities that family participates in for fun.

Education Success Percentages

My father received his AA in Electronics and my mother was a home maker but performed jobs in technology and attended college classes after her kids were grown for interest. She could also perform short hand. All of the family are avid readers.

My siblings and I received college degrees or certifications in all technical, medical, or finance professions. Our children have done the same.

Laidlaw Name Origin

The surname "Laidlaw" is of Scottish origin. It is believed to be locational, deriving from a place name in Scotland. The exact origin of the name is uncertain, but one possibility is that it comes from the village of Ladhope in Roxburghshire, Scotland. Another theory

suggests it may be derived from the Old English words "laege" meaning "low" or "lye" and "hlaw" meaning "hill" or "mound," suggesting a person who lived by a low hill or in a sheltered hollow.

Given its association with the Scottish Borders, where the Border Reivers were active, it's likely that the Laidlaw surname has connections to that region and its history. Over time, as families migrated and settled in different areas, the surname spread beyond its original locale.

As with many surnames, variations in spelling and pronunciation have occurred over the centuries, so you may encounter alternative spellings such as Ladlaw, Laidlow, or Ladlow

Doherty Name Origin

The surname "Doherty" has Irish origins and is derived from the Gaelic name "Ó Dochartaigh." The prefix "Ó" indicates "descendant of," while "Dochartaigh" is derived from the Gaelic word "dochartach," meaning "hurtful" or "obstructive."

The Doherty clan originated in County Donegal in the northwest of

Ireland and were historically associated with the territory of Inishowen. They were one of the leading families of the Cenél Conaill tribal grouping, which was one of the two main branches of the Northern Uí Néill dynasties in medieval Ireland.

The Dohertys were a powerful clan in Donegal and were involved in various conflicts and alliances throughout Irish history. They played significant roles in local politics, warfare, and the preservation of Gaelic culture.

As with many Irish surnames, the spelling and pronunciation of "Doherty" may vary, and you may encounter variations such as Dougherty or Docherty. THE BORDER REIVERS – history of some of our ancestors per the family name – Laidlaw – Scottish decent

Is Laidlaw A Border Reiver Name

Yes, "Laidlaw" is indeed associated with the Border Reivers, who were raiders along the Anglo-Scottish border in the late medieval period. The Reivers were notorious for their lawlessness and frequent raids on both sides of the border. Many families, including the Laidlaws, were part of this turbulent history. The Laidlaws were one of the Border Reiver families, known for their involvement in the raids and conflicts of the time.

Who Were The Border Reivers

The Border Reivers were inhabitants of the Anglo-Scottish borderlands, particularly during the late medieval and early modern periods, roughly from the 13th to the 17th centuries. They were known for their lawlessness, raiding, and general disorder along the border region between England and Scotland.

These were not formal armies or organized militias but rather extended families and clans who engaged in a cycle of raiding, plundering, and retaliatory violence. They exploited the lawless and disputed nature of the border region, which was often beyond the reach of central authority from either kingdom. This lawlessness persisted for centuries due to the ongoing conflicts between England and Scotland and the weak control of both monarchies over the border region.

The Reivers were skilled horsemen and fighters, often conducting lightning-fast raids known as "reiving" on both sides of the border. They targeted not only rival clans but also settlements and farms, stealing livestock, goods, and occasionally people for ransom or revenge.

Despite their reputation for lawlessness, the Border Reivers also had their own codes of conduct and systems of justice within their communities. Feuds between families could last for generations, with violence begetting more violence.

The Border Reiver era came to an end in the late 16th and early 17th centuries with the unification of the English and Scottish crowns under James VI of Scotland, who became James I of England. The centralization of authority and the imposition of law and order in the border region gradually suppressed the Reiver way of life, although their legacy continues to be remembered in the folklore, history, and surnames of the borderlands.

DNA Results Summary for Peter Laidlaw

O MapboJ(.e OprmSlun1tMap

Ethnicity Estimate

- Ireland — 70%
  - :t: Donegal, Ireland
    - :!: Inlshowen
  - :! Central Ireland
    - '!' North Leitrim & Bordering Counties
    - '!' North East Sligo & North Leitrim
- '.f: Munster, Ireland
  - · . Central Munster
  - ,'!: South West Munster
- Scotland — 22%
- Germanic Europe — 4%
- England & Northwestern Europe — 4%

(D
If.

Our Family Dynamics Concerns

There was a time not too long ago when each of us struggled and called upon our parents for help and support. We were never turned aside and helped in our own way by them. Upon their deaths, their message was to "take care of each other" in time of need.

Since their passing, our family can disintegrate into three types of groups if we don't stay vigilant:

The Want to Be's

Takers

Outcasts

The Want to Be's are the most successful in a monetary way. They have high paying jobs and surround themselves with phony friends who tell them how wonderful they are. They are under the illusion that their money gives them real power. They couldn't be further from the truth. They look down on others and believe they are better.

The takers are the ones who sit back and let everyone help them without regard to bettering themselves through effort. They "use" people to get what they want and need. They don't contribute to anything or anyone but themselves.

The outcasts are the ones who still believe in the values of the family and the lessons taught by their parents and other ancestors. Honor and respect are their weapons and loyalty to the family is without question. They will protect the family and help anyone by whatever means necessary. They fear no one regardless of money nor reputation. They don't exist in the Want to Be's or takers' world and are looked upon with fear and disdain.

We have come to a different road with the passing of our parents and siblings being stricken with sickness. Where do we go from here?

Please search your hearts and souls for the answers and remember a time when you needed help and it came to you. When people reach out to you, are you going to help them? Just remember that no matter where you are in life at this time, there were others who sacrificed to put you there. Never forget where you came from!

If you truly want to have the family we all talk about, it will take effort from all of us to make it that way. If you choose to be too busy or your life is more important than other family members, then don't be surprised at the outcome. As we all get older, it would be nice to have somebody with us when we move on to meet our maker rather than being alone due to our choices. What are you prepared to do?

Our Society

Our Present Society

The society we live in now is quite different than when we grew up. The technology has opened up so many more opportunities for knowledge and education. However, it has also affected the way we communicate as human beings.

Many people have become withdrawn and would rather text or email someone rather than speak with them face to face. This is the first lesson to you. If you have a real problem with someone and need to speak to them about an issue, go to their house or meet them face to face and talk it out. We are emotional creatures and speaking to each other directly you can sense facial expressions and body language. It is also easier to know when to control your voice and back off if necessary. People who text and can't speak with you directly don't always get the meaning correctly at times which can become misinterpreted.

Our Society Lies

They glamorize people with no class.

They guilt you into not being good enough through advertising (TV/internet/cell phone apps/etc.)

Everything is a big hurry and you are constantly pushed.

Some people with big money don't really understand how much the majority of people struggle to survive. They can't relate.

There are others however who do a great job to help the human race. They are not all blind.

Family Code

Loyalty At All Times – Blood is thicker than water.

Loyalty to the family should be without question. It is the duty of every man and woman of our bloodline to never disgrace our family name in any way. Should someone break this sacred right, then their punishment should fit what is justified by the members of the family.

Never Bring People Into The Group That Are Suspect.

You are represented by the people surrounding you. If you bring a person into our group that is a problem, then they will be dealt with first. After that, you will be next.

Deeds Not Words – don't talk about doing it, make it happen

My father used to use this term a lot. He would say "Don't talk about getting something done. Do it!" So many people say a lot of things and never do them. Don't be one of them. Set your goals and go after your dreams!

Never Sell Out A Family Member/Never give up anyone in the family – never disclose anything to anyone. Let the issue be handled from within. A lot of this is due to interpretation. It depends upon the circumstances in most difficult cases. Find out what happened first in any situation before jumping into action. Get all the facts and the best way to protect the person before doing anything foolish.

Never Concede Defeat – don't allow nor show people you are beaten. Regroup your efforts to create success. You are not always going to win in everything you do. However, reassess what made you lose or fail, so it will be easier to face once again in a different way and with better results. You learn how to win by facing the agony of losing.

No Excuses – the world can be a cruel place. Don't make excuses why you can't do something. Find out what is needed to get the task completed. My father used to use the line "Hard work and Discipline". I must have heard it a million times growing up as a kid. What he was telling me was this: If I did work hard and discipline myself to accomplish what I set goals for, then I would never have to make excuses. Excuses are for people who are either in terrible circumstances and can't get out or lazy. There are a lot of people who don't want to put in the work to be what they want or get what they want.

Secrecy – Keep all family actions within the group. Don't disclose information to others outside the group. It keeps things safer.

Positive Role Model – Think as smart, athletic, tough, etc. use your natural ability to be the best. Assist the weak and always have an exceptional attitude.

Teamwork Always – no matter what your success level, you represent the group. Each day you go out in the world, it is expected that you will act and behave accordingly. Do not use your individuality for doing wrong. When people see you, it is as a representative of the group. Don't bring a negative light on us by your actions.

Different From Others – We are different than other people. Not from a conceited or arrogant standpoint. We stand out naturally to other people. Use this ability for good and do not allow others to put you down or become jealous because of it. Don't hate me because you aren't me!

When You're Out, You're Out. You are welcome to join – Follow the code and you can remain a part of the family forever. If you are blood and you mess up, you will be judged by the family. If you are not blood and mess up badly, you will be asked to leave and you will not be allowed to return. Ever. This may not sound like such a big deal to some, but others will beg their whole lives to come back. We have a great family and want those coming in to know that.

Never Disown Anyone In The Family. This is an open ended point. You have to follow the family code or guidelines. You can't run wild and get into trouble and expect your family to bail you out. There has to be some kind of morals and ethics that everyone should follow. We have had people get arrested and had alcohol and drug problems. We have fought in wars and had to take lives to survive. We are not saints. However, that doesn't give you the right to tarnish our name just because you feel like it. If you break the law you have to be able to handle the consequences that go with it.

Wealth Does Not Ensure Class. Just because you have money doesn't mean your better than everyone. This message is for the future generations. All of the people in this family now have worked extremely hard to get in the financial position they have currently. They do not however speak down to people and think they are better because they understand what it took to get where they are now. You are expected to do the same.

You Represent Everyone In The Family, Not Just Yourself. When you go out in the world you are expected to set a good example for others and represent your people well. When you do it makes our family look good to others. When you don't not only do you make yourself look bad but the family as well.

Work Hard And Discipline Yourself To Achieve Your Goals. Use every avenue that is available to become the best version of yourself. There is no other way to fulfill your destiny without putting in the effort to do so. Set goals to keep you on track. Once it has been accomplished set another one. Perseverance is the key to success. You have to keep trying over and over until you get to where you want and need to be.

You Are Judged By Those You're Surrounded By. Make good choices. Your success in life depends upon the people you surround yourself with. If you surround yourself with motivated and good people, chances are high that you will become the same. If you surround yourself with unmotivated and bad people you can become like them. Our ancestors made tremendous sacrifices to put us in a better position to improve ourselves and the world around us. Hang out with the right people and not the wrong ones.

Honor Yourself And Ancestors. Never forget where you came from. Be the best that you can be in whatever you do. Be a great example to other people. There are people who sacrificed much to put you where you are today. Make them proud. Make a difference in the world.

Be The Best. Don't sell yourself short. You have been given talents that nobody else possesses but yourself. You owe it to yourself and others to find out what they are and use them. Work hard and your efforts will pay off.

What Matters Is What You Think About Yourself. There will be people who try to put you down. They will try to make you look bad and say things about you that are not true. Don't listen to them. Keep working hard everyday to improve yourself. Follow your dreams and your sixth sense. They will guide you on your path to success.

We Have Been Taught And Raised Correctly. You are surrounded by a great family. We were raised by people who want to see us succeed. This book is filled with ways to live the right way and be an upbeat positive human being. Your ancestors sacrificed their lives to create a good family. Use these teachings to assist future generations.

We Are Equal To Other Races And Them To Us. The biggest struggle in the world for thousands of years was the concept that some people were better than others. It has been the cause of wars, famine, disease, health, and peace. I hope that future generations can see past this and create a world everyone can live in. No more hunger, death, greed, hatred. Impossible you say? We never even tried it yet.

What We Do In This World Matters. Every person born into this world is here for a reason. It doesn't matter the circumstances. God has a plan for you. You just have to figure out what it is. The things that you do make a difference in this world. Don't sell yourself short. We all can't be president but we can save or contribute in any way we can. One person can do a lot if they put the effort into it. Make a difference in what you do. No matter what it is someone will gain something from it.

We Never Mistake Kindness For Weakness. Just because you are nice doesn't give people the right to walk all over you. It is okay to stand up to them and tell them you will not be disrespected. Bring a good person doesn't mean people can treat you badly. That is unacceptable.

We Never Allow Others To Talk Down To Us Or Disrespect Our Way Of Life. Every person has the right to live the way they feel will benefit them. However, that doesn't give you the right to dump on how we choose to live. We were raised the correct way. We will not allow you to put down our way of life just because you don't agree with it.

Everyone Has The Capacity To Change. Don't buy into the line when people say they can't change or won't because they're satisfied with their behavior. Nonsense. Everyone should strive to change themselves regularly to become a better person and help the world. Those that don't are just lying to themselves.

Our Women Are Equal - They educate themselves, raise children and work like us, so forget the old-fashioned ways of mankind. The idea that gives us the best plan for opportunity to succeed can come from all of us and not just male members of the family. They are wise beyond their years. Listen to them. They keep the entire family focused on what is right and how to love and control our emotions. We would fail without them.

Never Make Foolish Mistakes That Embarrass The Family - You are to maintain control when outside in the real world. Never drink or party outside the home unless it is a minimal amount of one. You need to be able to get yourself home without help. Keep your habits within your own domain.

Kids Advice

Do not touch or play with anything that is not yours.

Do not disturb others when they are sleeping unless it's an emergency.

Do not wander into other people's rooms unless permitted.

We do not hide from others.

Speak your mind and do not whisper or keep secrets from each other.

If there is information you are not ready to receive due to your age it will be discussed away from you so there is no confusion.

Do not lie! Tell the truth always!

Do not steal. Don't take something that does not belong to you. Ever!

Respect all things in the home, including the animals. You are a guest and expected to behave accordingly.

Behave your elders. They are wiser than you are at this time. They have more experience than you do.

Everyone in the family is equal. No one is more special than the other. Your talents and abilities are your own and make you special. We are all special in our own way. Embrace it!

Keep your room clean.

Everything you have has been given to you. It can also be taken away as well

You are expected to behave. If you act up, you will be punished.

All rules set forth and agreed upon by all apply to everyone and you are expected to heed them

When you go out in public you represent the family. You are expected to be strong, smart, and caring to others. Look people in the eye and not at the ground. Be confident and represent us well!

Words To Understand When Young:

Manipulation — the ability to make others do what you want them to. Our family knows and understands when someone else is trying to do it to them. We understand how to work with human beings and do not trick them into getting what we want.

Trust – if I can't trust what you do or say it is going to be difficult for us to get along very well.

Respect – if you do not respect your elders than why should they respect you. Never mistake their kindness for weakness.

Loyalty/Obedience – loyalty to the family is without question. We do the right things to make our family and all of us the most powerful people we can on this earth. We do good and not evil. We help each other and the people we can along the way.

Punishment – there are consequences to pay if you break the rules and you will be held accountable for your actions. Don't test your elders or you will not like the result.

Our Way Of Life

We are different, not better or below others.

We have been taught and raised correctly.

We are equal to other races and them to us.

What we do in this world matters.

We never mistake kindness for weakness.

We never allow others to talk down to us or disrespect our way of life.

Motivational Statements

Deeds not words.

Defeat is not an option.

Rest your face and hands.

Never mistake kindness for weakness.

Hard work and discipline.

If you are going to do it, don't just do it halfway but 150 percent.

Twice as smart, twice as tough, twice as good at everything.

Don't ever give up.

It won't happen in your time; it will happen in God's time.

Defiant till the end.

Always expect to win, never think of losing.

Never concede defeat.

Never allow people to defeat you.

Life is hard for everyone, not just you.

Don't lower yourself to their standards, bring them up to yours.

When they look in your eyes they have to believe.

Our System

We do not have this entire system in place now but there are parts of it. Our future existence may depend on adding additional parts to it mentioned below:

5 To 7 People Council – Equal Input

The family council should meet monthly or quarterly to discuss ways to improve the quality of life for all members of the family. Generate ideas or experiences on ways to make each family member stronger.

Scottish Or Irish Clan Mentality – Combine Families

Surround ourselves with the right people. If each family brings in ten quality people and you get twenty quality family members to support all of them then you have two hundred people looking to improve our chances of success. This is a low example of what could happen. I believe it could be much larger.

Family Guidelines Importance Of

All family members have equal say in all matters. Age, sex, education, wealth should have no bearing on who is part of the family council. The best people should be on the council to preserve our right as Laidlaw's to live on this earth.

No ideas or choices shall be forced on any family member. Each person has the right to their own decisions. However, if the decision is incorrect then that person has to take complete ownership and accept the consequences.

We have been pushing away at times rather than uniting. We have to make each other stronger. We have to share skills to make the council and the rest of the family stronger. The better we all are the stronger we can make the family become successful.

Promoting Each Other

We are the key! Network each other into higher positions of power as well as other members of the family. High positions create more money, investments and a chance at stock options.

Our strengths

Intelligence

Charm

Work experience

Drive

Motivation

Salesmanship

Reputation

Building Our Own Future.

The success of the family is based on everyone doing their best to become as talented and powerful as possible. These abilities will make it easier for future generations to learn and build upon.

Funding For Elders.

The older people get in the family the more assistance they may need. Most families within the family have been willing to assist their parents or brothers and sisters when possible. This has been pretty consistent over the years and recommended it for the generations following next.

Monthly Meetings.

My suggestion has been to build a council of people to assist the family. If agreed upon there should be monthly meetings to see where everything stands.

Political Ambitions.

We have some bright and talented people in the family. It should not be considered far fetched to get into the political arena. If real changes are to take place in the world by concerned people that would be a good place to start.

Eliminating Negative Thoughts.

This is a tough one. We are surrounded by negative people on a daily basis. I call it the doom and gloom mindset. It is difficult to get by on our daily tasks without allowing negative thoughts to control us. Stay positive and everything will work out.

Using Natural Abilities

Creating revenue in our family. Everyone has a purpose in this life. Find out what you are good at and use those abilities to better your life. If you don't know right away try different things to see what you are good at or can do easily without much effort.

Use the natural abilities of our family members to create or design something that people want

Take classes that you enjoy and may use to create a career path

Find out what people really want and need and provide it for them

Key Words

These subjects are covered in various sections of the book. The list is placed here to add additional subject matter for the future without duplication.

Old Ways Words To Live By

Anger

This is one of the most difficult emotions to control. People can do things that want to make you fly off the handle. The old saying is true. Never argue with an idiot for they will drag you down to their level and beat you up with years of experience.

Charity

There are so many ways to help others. It doesn't always have to be with a monetary donation. Volunteering your time and experience is also a form of charity. The world needs help. Pick a place and go for it. You not only help others but yourself as well.

Crying

Crying should never be seen as a sign of weakness. It is the bodies way of releasing energy. No man or woman will ever be seen differently by weeping. Some people cry and others do not. My mother told me if it hurts cry. It is necessary at times.

Dancing

One of the best releases of tension and energy is dancing. People say they can't dance. Ridiculous. Get up and move around and have fun. Who cares what you think you look like. Have a little enjoyment and cut loose. Dance as if nobody is watching. When alone at home put on some music and dance. You don't always need a partner. I used to dance with my dog. She thought I was crazy by the look on her face.

Defeat

There are times when we are all going to get knocked down. My mother told me life is liking a boxing match. You're going to get knocked down to the canvas. Each time you have to get back up and get back in the fight again.

Defiance

There is a stubbornness that most of us in this family are born with. It is hard to figure out where it comes from but it is there in all of us. We are a people that do not like to be controlled in our decisions. Does that mean we are inflexible? No, it means "we're confident in our ability to make the correct choices without the pressure of outside influence. Some will see this as arrogance. It is not. You have to be confident in what you are doing even if others are trying to tell you not to do them.

Desire

When you eliminate the desire for something in your mind, it also cures the obsession of it.

Divorce

Many of my family members have been affected by divorce including myself. Sometimes people grow apart from each other. They can get real ugly and the person you thought you knew is nothing like who you started with. They will lie and say terrible things about you. Accuse you of having done things that never happened. The saddest thing is how it affects the children. You have to find the strength to move on. If people want out of your life let them go. They were not meant to finish life's journey with you. In most cases they did you a favor by leaving. There is another purpose for you now. I attended a program called "Divorce Care" which changed my life. Perhaps it can help others as well.

Duty

It is your duty to your ancestors and family to live up to a certain standard and if people are going to be a part your life they have to as well.

Education

"The only way to better yourself is to be educated." This was told to me by my mother. Her grandfather said it was essential that each generation improve the next and that one of the ways to do this was to gain knowledge through education. Many of the people in my family have made significant progress in their lives through gaining diplomas or certifications in different areas of skill. Others have been trained in certain trades that allowed them more flexibility to learn to work on building homes, electrical, plumbing and heating and air conditioning. Other fields to include auto mechanic, assisting people in cosmetology and health care positions. Learning new things is the key to improving one's self and becoming successful. We have been very fortunate to have great teachers. One of the things you will always remember is a great teacher. Bad bosses, relationships, friends you will easily forget but not a person who took the time to improve you as a person.

Our education system has changed a great deal. Teachers are more baby sitters then educators. Kids are going through the motions and not really getting the information they really need. We need to set up a system to improve this. One of the things that I wanted to suggest was a class on manners. When you think about it, how sad is it that kids can not behave themselves. In most cases you would hope that parents were holding their kids accountable and creating some type of consequences. That is the way it was when I was growing up as a kid. My son had a suggestion that if he was a teacher he would inform his students and parents that if they were not interested in putting the effort into his class then just don't attend. If teachers take the time to actually teach, then it is up to the students to listen. When their parents asked why their child was failing then it would be disclosed to them because their child never came to class.

My father was kind of a stickler about our getting a high school diploma but it didn't click at the time. He finally confessed that he did not get his high school diploma because he enlisted in the Air Force during WWII prior to graduating. He felt it was more important to protect the country and would finish his degree "if" he came back. He was a highly decorated war hero flying in some incredible air missions and he was still worried about us graduating. He later gained an AA in electronics and was an accomplished engineer for over 30 years. "Hard Work and Discipline" he used to say. Must have heard it a million times. Heck of a father, I miss him every day.

Family

Next to God, the most valuable 2nd thing in my life is my family. My dad used to say, "you can always get a new job but you can't always get a new family."

Health

Everything in moderation, nothing in excess. Take care of yourself physically and mentally. Train your whole life. It saved mine when I had health issues as I got older. Doctor said I would have died if I wasn't in good shape.

Holidays

My favorite time of the year is from September to December. That is when all the major holidays kick in. It starts with Halloween in October, Thanksgiving in November, Christmas in December, and the beginning of the new year in January. The weather is always changing as well. The air gets a little cooler and the environment changes from the trees going into hibernation and the beauty of the colors all around us.

There has been much controversy created in the past few years about the celebration of all of the different holidays. There is a very simple solution to this. In our society there are many diverse cultures. When growing up in Massachusetts as a child we celebrated Halloween, Thanksgiving, Christmas, and New Year's during the fall and winter months. These were considered staple holidays. They never changed. If people choose not to celebrate these particular holidays that is fine. That also goes for other holidays throughout the year. If other people feel that they want to celebrate different or additional holidays feel free to do so. However, don't ruin it for everyone else. If one person does want to be involved, then don't allow them to create a situation where the majority of people are punished for taking part in that holiday.

Halloween is not a demonic event. It was created for children to go from house to house to receive candy. Kids get the opportunity to dress up in different ways to have fun. Some of these outfits are scary but that is all part of how Halloween is set up. If others do not want to participate in this event fine. The evil that they create is within themselves and not the activity. To put fear in the hearts of young children and adults about this festivity is just plain wrong. Kids in some places are not allowed to wear costumes to school because it may offend others. Get over it. It's one day. Stop trying to take away the fun from people.

Hope 1

When I was a young man my father asked me what I wanted to do in my life. I told him I wanted to get a good job, make some money, and possibly start a family with children one day. He said that was a good plan. He also said what about everybody else in the world? Aren't you going to think of other people as well? He told me the most important thing you can give a person is hope. You can't solve all their problems but a word of encouragement can go a long way. If you see another human struggle, try and lift their spirits with a word of praise or a joke to make them laugh and lighten their spirits. Sometimes that's all they need to keep going that day.

Kindness

Never mistake kindness for weakness

Some of the toughest people I have ever met were some of the nicest. Let people know that just because you're being nice doesn't mean they can walk all over you.

Life

Life isn't always fair and it's all about the money in most situations my father used to say. Everything in some way revolves around money. People will sell their souls for it. Enjoy life and get the most out of it without giving up too much.

Loyalty

Loyalty is not only being true to the people around you, but to your own self.

Should never be sold for any price.

To give the best of yourself for other people to change yourself and others around you.

To be able to stand by yourself and your beliefs no matter what the consequences.

A true leader will gain loyalty through their people first.

Loyalty, like love, is a strong emotion. Without one, you could not have the other. They are true friends.

Manners

It separates us from the beasts of the world. You can be charming and somebody to be taken seriously. The roughest people in the world knew it that's why they didn't waste time proving it. Gentlemen and ladies are few and far between these days. We need to resurrect a time when people had class and practiced courtesy. Impossible you say, maybe, but let's set the example. Show the people of the world how they should act.

Money

Everybody needs it to survive. Some people are obsessed by it and can never get enough. Some get by with very little. It is necessary to obtain the basics of food, clothing and shelter. The only advice I can give is don't let it only define you by having more. Since I have never been in the status of having a great deal of it there is only so much I can say about it. It doesn't cure loneliness, depression or unhappiness though. Even those with more don't have the easiest lives. Lastly, somebody is always trying to take it away from you. That would be exhausting.

Negativity

Parents teach their children today

You are better than they are

You don't have to be accountable for what you do

Poor

So what does it mean to grow up poor. I grew up in a large family. Money was tight but there was a lot of love. My parents were very supportive but stressed hard work and discipline to achieve the things you want in life. Times were hard but it made me a better person. It's easy to make excuses of why you can't do something because of your environment. Push yourself to be the best person you can regardless of your status.

Protection

This a very sensitive area because you don't want to come over as aggressive towards other people. This is a basic survival mindset that is shared by most human beings and their families. The question should never be should I get involved. You are expected to jump in and take action so the question never has to be raised at any time. Each male shall fight to the bitter end to protect each other and the women and children of the family unit. Our women and children are powerful in their own right and may assist in the protection of the family. If by yourself, and outnumbered you must inflict pain on those who would do harm to you, our women and children until your last breath. Our men, women and children should never use this protection against others without cause. It should never be compromised to gain favor or attention from others. If a person is causing an issue they will be dealt with at certain levels of discipline.

Reality

If I wanted what you have, I would have taken it already.

Religion

This is always a touchy subject for most people. No matter what you say, most or some people aren't going to like it. The best advice from me would be to check them all out. That does not mean you have to change the one you are a member of now. I took a class called "Religion in America" in college where we looked at all of the religions. It is difficult to find fault with something if you take the time to see what it is about rather than making a statement based on no fact at all.

We had to write a term paper on religion other than our own. I went to a Japanese Buddhist Temple for two consecutive Sundays. It was so different but enlightening just the same. I was even fortunate to talk with one of their priests and he explained about the religion and what they believed. What is truly amazing is how close each religion is to each other in terms of meaning and how it is applied to everyday life.

So what is my message? Think for yourself. Don't allow anyone to tell you how to believe. Believe in what is the truth in your eyes. Keep your soul as clean and untainted as long as you can. Follow your instincts and make your own decisions. Learning about other religions is not wrong and may even improve your perspective on other people and what they believe. Be responsible. Don't blame God or anyone else for your situation. Do something about it. No excuses. Ask God and the powers of the universe for help. Go after what you want in life.

Respect

Never forget the generations of people that came before you and where you come from. No matter how successful you become in your life remember those who sacrificed everything to put you in that position. Your ancestors should always be in your memory for they helped you become what you are today.

Responsibility

Loyalty to the Laidlaw family should be without question. It is the responsibility of every man and woman of our bloodline to never disgrace our family name in anyway. You not only represent yourself when you go out in the world but every member of our family. Should someone break this sacred right than their punishment should fit what is justified by other members of the family.

Rich

So what does it mean to grow up rich. Do they really have it better than the common person? They seem to have just as many problems as anyone else. They can't escape drug addition, abuse, prejudice. Many do help people in need. It would be nice to have all people of whatever their background is to come together to make this a better world. Is that too much to ask for. Perhaps not.

Satisfaction

In our society today, it is sometimes very difficult to satisfy the wants and needs of another person; due to the fact that other person you are trying to please does not truly understand their own wants and needs on how to be satisfied.

The Old Ways Philosophies

Don't Settle – Balance

Don't settle for certain people in your life and just try and fit in. Surround yourself with positive, motivated, and upbeat people and not those that treat you badly and tell you all the things you do wrong. Don't allow them to drag you down to their level. It is better to be with fewer good friends than a bunch of idiots who don't care about you at all and never will.

Have Class And Live By It - Class

Class is always acting accordingly in a variety of different situations. It is controlling your inner emotions and using the correct opinions and responses when others fail to do so. You are not born with it and cannot buy it as some people believe. It has to be acquired through self-discipline and saying and doing the appropriate things even when others don't.

Have Compassion For Others – Compassion

There are people out there who have suffered more than can be imagined. Their lives have been extremely difficult since they were born. Their pain is real and they are just looking for some understanding. Sometimes all it takes is a kind word or a small deed of help to make them feel wanted. They never asked to be in this situation it just happened. Remember this and show them the kindness you would hope to receive if you were in their place.

Responsibility For Your Actions - Consequences

Consequences are the price you pay for doing something wrong. You own up to your mistake and take responsibility for it.

Be Courageous - Courage

Fear is an emotion that sometimes prevents you from taking the steps you've always wanted to but were unsure of. Push it aside and do the things you were born to do and open yourself up to unlimited possibilities.

Criticism Rarely Works - Criticism

Nobody likes to be criticized. There are other words you can use to get the same point across. Once something is said in anger or frustration it can't be taken back easily. Take the time necessary to find them within before speaking and respect from others will be yours always.

Parent Fairly - Fairness

Being a parent is the most difficult thing you will ever do in your life. There are no real rule books on how to be a good one. It requires patience, sacrifice, and the ability to listen. You are the role model your children will follow as an example. Be fair in all decisions made and do it right the first time for you may not get another chance. When your children make a mistake they have to understand the consequences of their acts or decisions. When you make a mistake you need to admit it to them and apologize. That is how you maintain a common bond between both of you that will never break.

Be Who You Are - Fear

Don't be afraid to be yourself. If you were meant to make others laugh do it. If you were meant to give others hope do it. If you were meant to provide understanding to those in need do it. By giving of yourself to others the rewards received back are priceless.

Communicate With Others - Focus

Open up the lines of communication between others. Go outside and meet and greet your neighbors. There are risks in putting yourself out there but someone has to take the first step. Your own intuition will guide you in this endeavor.

Appreciation Of Friendship - Friendship

It amazes me how so many people will take advantage of their friendship with others. Instead of looking at me as an equal, they automatically think after a period of time that they are in control. How amusing. Did you honestly believe at any time you were in control? That is the question you should be asking yourself.

Friendship is not a right. It is a privilege. The people you surround yourself with have to be epic. Each of you showing respect to each other, taking care of business, no fools and no troublemakers. We protect each other as brothers and sisters in the same cause. It is tiring to see high level people looking to control us. Race, gender, creed and physical appearance should not matter. Unite for a common cause together with one goal as a marker. Freedom is not free. Honor your ancestors!

Lighten Up - Fun

Being serious all the time can be downright boring. Loosen yourself up and have fun by doing the things you really enjoy whether others think they are cool or not.

Belief In The Future Generations - Generations

It has been told to me that the next generation doesn't stand a chance because their outlook of the world is so negative. I do not believe that. They just haven't been taught to live by a certain code or been around the right people. I hope to change their outlook from teachings and experiences in my life from past generations to me.

Set Goals In Your Life – Goals

Set goals for what you want to accomplish each day and get them completed. Be realistic as to what you can get done in the time that you have. Have a well thought out plan for the future so that you will have a road map on how to get there. To truly gain happiness in your life you have to know what you want and how to achieve it.

Have Gratitude For Everything - Gratitude

Be grateful for everything you have. Your family and friends are the ones who are reminders to be thankful for their love and support which keeps you going through the tough times.

Eliminate Guilt – Guilt

Guilt trips last way too long. Forgive yourself and others and take your next vacation to a place called happiness.

Being Honest – Honesty

Honesty is asking someone you hold in high regard what they think of you or a situation that you are in and they respond by telling you how they truly feel.

Provide Hope To Others - Hope

Hope is one of the most powerful things you can award to others. It gives them the courage to move forward in their lives and they will never forget you for providing it to them when they needed it most.

Make Your Ancestors Proud - Honor

Never forget where you came from. The ancestors that made the moves and changes in their lives to put you in the position you are in now should never be forgotten. It is your duty to honor them by being the best person that you can be. Always do the right thing no matter what level in society you attain to.

Stay United - Justice

Unity is the key to mankind surviving. For thousands of years there has been a movement that has pit us against each other. All of our people have suffered at the hands of those who wish to do us harm. We have to have the courage to let go of the past and set aside our differences and come together as one human race. It will be our gift to the future generations that come after us.

Sense Of Humor - Laughter

Making others laugh is addicting. The release of pent up energy provides a sense of relief that their body cherishes more than one can imagine or describe.

Justice For People - Laws

Justice is when the input from the law abiding citizens from all backgrounds decides the laws that were set up to protect them are weak or can be manipulated. The laws are democratically voted on and changed so that the villains are severely punished and the common person no longer has to distance themselves from each other.

Leadership

"When they look in your eyes they have to believe."

There are many managers out there but very few leaders. A leader takes the time to see how everyone else is doing within the group. They are not overly concerned about their own path for they feel that there will be time to figure that out themselves. A leader listens to what people have to say about certain situations. They may not always agree but listen just the same.

Anyone that is only interested in bettering themselves can never be a true leader. It requires sacrifice, dedication, humility and doing the right thing. Leaders are not just made they are born to do it. Many of you will notice people in our society that are just natural leaders. It comes easy to them and many people are drawn to them because of this ability.

It was a difficult decision in writing this book because the responsibility of being a leader was placed on me. You are placed in a situation where there is a good chance that you will be criticized for what you believe and not everyone is going to agree with you.

My father was a great leader. He took the time to get involved in different organizations and people. He was a boy scout, little league, and band leader. His relationship with all the people in those groups was incredible. They didn't always agree with what my father said but respected his honesty and guidance in difficult times and situations.

Many of you reading this book will find yourselves in the same situation. There will be times as parents or on an individual basis that you will be asked to step into this role. You not only owe it to yourself but to others to participate. There is always hesitation with giving of one's self to improve matters but you cannot always depend upon others to do it. Believe in yourself and do the best that you can. That is all anyone can ask of you.

Appreciate Love - Love

Love is one of the most powerful emotions if not "the" most powerful. To love someone and be loved in return is unbelievable because it affects each person differently. Cherish it for as long as you can for finding people like that in your life can leave you with fond memories to last you forever.

Teach Your Children - Parenting

Children are the greatest gift you can ever have in life. When they make a mistake or do something wrong take the time to explain to them what it is they did incorrectly. Raising your voice and punishing them without their understanding why only limits their ability to learn and make corrections in the future. Remember, they are children and have to be taught. Parenting or supporting a child takes lots of time and patience. Pick your battles carefully. They are expected to make errors and mistakes. Just like we did.

Loyalty To Country - Patriotism

Patriotism is standing up and protecting the ideals that you and those around you believe in against those that want to take them away.

Peace Within Family - Peace

Make every effort to make peace with others in your family. No matter how crazy they drive you cherish the time together. For when they are gone you will never be able to get those moments back ever again.

Be Unique - Perfection

Perfection is something that our society pushes on us each day in regards to physical beauty, family, how you act, etc. It's funny that your little imperfections are the things that make you unique from others and allow you to stand out in a positive way to people. Embrace them, for that is why they were given to you in the first place.

You Are Here For A Reason - Purpose

Take heart that you were born into this world for a purpose and to provide help to someone. There may be times when you feel alone but do not despair. If you were not here for an opportunity to do something wonderful you would never exist in the first place. Find your purpose and make the world a better place. You will always count for something no matter what you do. Make us proud.

The Value Of Friendship - Relationships

True friendship consists of two essential things, the good news and the bad news. The good news is easy because you can tell them the wonderful things they are doing. The bad news is tough because you have to look them in the eye and tell them what they are doing wrong and why you disagree with it. Can't have one without the other.

Live By A Code Of Conduct - Rules

A code of conduct is a set of rules that has been passed down from within a family to its members for generations. They guide you in the proper way of living even when society falters and becomes weak and easily corrupted. The code encourages acts such as bravery, respect, trust, loyalty and honor and is not negotiable. When you live by a code you are held accountable for your actions and it can never be taken away unless you allow others to break it. It may bend during trials in your life but will never break if you follow its guidelines.

Share Wisdom With Others – Sharing

Relationships with people outside your family can be complicated. They may have been raised in a different manner and discussing your family code or way of doing things to them may open their eyes to a world they have never been a part of.

Be Accountable – Standards

Some people are being held accountable for things they do and others are not. That is one reason why our society is so messed up. It begins within your own family in correcting the problem. Instead of trying to blame others and point fingers clean up the issues in your own home. Stop trying to deflect away your responsibility by attempting to fix other people's problems and solve your own.

The Importance Of Loyalty - Support

Respect plus trust equals loyalty. When you gain one's respect, you gain their trust. When you gain their trust, you gain their loyalty. When you gain their loyalty they will do most anything for you. And you will do the same for them.

Trust Your Children - Trust

Trust your children's judgements. Allow them to make some of their own decisions as they get older and grow. It will teach them to learn from the choices made whether right or wrong. They will always ask you for guidance but realize that you will not be on this earth forever. By preparing them now you are readying them to take on the world when you are gone.

Think For Yourself - Thinking

Don't believe all the lies they want you to fear via social media or TV. Instead live your life by a code of conduct that has been passed down from generation to generation for many years that cannot be broken by anyone unless you allow it to.

Unity Towards Each Other – Unity

Unity is the key to mankind surviving. For thousands of years there has been a movement that has pit us against each other. Call it evil, sin or the anti-Christ but all of our people have suffered at the hands of those who wish to do us harm. We have to have the courage to let go of the past and set aside our differences and come together as one human race. It will be our gift to the future generations that come after us.

Family Name Value - Value

Your family name is one of the most priceless things that you have. To tarnish it in any way is to bring insult to those in your family now and those who came before you who strived to keep it noble.

Be Wise In Your Thinking - Wisdom

Wisdom can be gained from those of all ages. You will meet people that are older and act or behave less mature and those that are younger that act or behave more mature. Don't close your mind to people of different generations for you really don't know what their lives were like before you met them and how much they can teach you or you can teach them.

My Terms

From this day forward, I will modify my way of life. I have tried to be kind and decent to people my whole life. I will still do this for most people, but not for everyone.

If people do not want to be a part of my life, so be it. I will spend the rest of my days happy whether that be by myself or with another.

I will be very selective of the people I surround myself with. I will eliminate all negative thoughts in my brain with meditation and Tai Chi. Prayer will drive me.

I will be a God-fearing man. He will reveal my next purpose in life after healing all aspects of my body and mind.

You are a good man! Some people do not deserve you in their lives! Don't fret over it any longer.

Do not waste time with people you rarely see or are not contacted by. It is energy that can be used somewhere else.

Do not chase people. If they approach you than speak with them openly. If they do not, then let them go. You can't please everyone. Some of them will try to take advantage of your kindness. Don't give them an edge to use against you.

What I Believe In

God

Jesus Christ

Most people are good, their decisions may not be

True Love

Friends Forever

Work Hard

Family

Honor

Doing the right thing

Great examples to our youth

Learning from mistakes

Being kind to others

Don't allow people to say bad things or treat you poorly

Mean what you say

Helping others

Being yourself

Using your abilities

Never laying down for anyone

Fighting for your beliefs

Have confidence

Accepting who you are

Be courageous in all things

Things I Don't Like

Arrogant people

Bad drivers

Cheapskates

Those that hurt others

Liars

Cheaters

People who steal

Laziness

Excuses by others

Poor sports

Bullies

Fakes or phonies

Constantly late people

Big mouths

Most lawyers, politicians, and priests

Mind games

People who think they are always smarter. Know it all's

Braggers

Negative people

People who try to put others down

Great Books I Have Read

Bible

How to stop worrying and start living – Dale Carnegie

What color is your Parachute?

The Art of War – Sun Tzu

Classics – Moby Dick, Robinson Crusoe, Animal Farm, Fahrenheit 451, Oliver Twist etc.

Murder mysteries

Any technical or non-technical "Dummies" books

Science fiction

Historical stories fiction and non-fiction

Sports stories

Detective stories

Comic books

Readers digest

Magazines

Cook books

How to draw books

All modern and older authors

Horror stories

Autobiography

Sherlock Holmes

Perry Mason

Encyclopedias

Great authors throughout history

Who Was He?

He was born into a wonderful family.

He was raised by wise parents.

He was fortunate to have great siblings.

He was surrounded by fantastic friends.

He was a good athlete.

He was a good student.

He was a member of the military.

He was given the opportunity to attend college and graduate.

He was married.

He was blessed with three beautiful children.

He was hired by successful companies his whole career.

He was able to travel across the country several times.

He was able to have great vacations in many places.

He was fortunate to live and reside in multiple states.

He was able to save a little money.

He was able to buy some nice things.

He was able to buy homes to live in.

He was influenced at times to use alcohol and drugs to deal with the pressures of life.

He was blessed with six grandchildren.

He was given the opportunity to share multiple experiences with his children and grandchildren.

He was divorced.

He was subjected to the COVID virus four times and survived.

He was partially paralyzed due to a herniated disk in his neck.

He was on the operating table and almost lost his life twice.

He was given the opportunity to live.

He was given the chance to bond with his family.

He was given the chance to grow wise from his children's advice.

He was given the chance to change as a person.

He was given the chance to train and rebuild his depleted body.

He was given the opportunity to help others.

He was given the chance to laugh again.

He was given the chance to love again.

He was given the chance to have fun again.

He was able to learn so many things in his life by himself and from others.

He was given the chance to be happy and to share it with others.

He was given the chance to make changes in his life when things needed to be corrected or to move on to different opportunities. Who is this lucky guy? ME

Preparing For The Future – My Children And Future Generations

1. Obtain personal property. - have owned and sold three houses in my life. First property tripled in value of what I paid for it. Other two properties doubled in value. Didn't gain those profits because had to sell early. However, if you can purchase property and hold on to it consider it a good long term investment. You will make money. I broke even on one property and made money on the other two

2. Life insurance - highly underrated. It is an excellent thing to have to protect your family. Should something happen it leaves your family with something to build from.

3. Investment accounts - invest at least 5 percent of your salary in a Roth or traditional 401 K plan. Over a number of years, it will grow in value.

 4. Savings - try and save 5 percent of your salary in savings. Have an emergency fund just in case.

5. Debt - read Dave Ramsey's book on paying off debt. The less debt you have the more money you keep.

6. Credit - having good credit is very important. If you are trying to purchase a home or car you will need it.

Listed below is an example of the direction my kids have taken to improve their lives and to grow in their careers. They have been involved in sports, cheer leading, dance and other activities helping them learn the concept of teamwork and getting along with others I have always asked them to have a plan to follow to obtain the things they wanted in life. There are families who have very successful children and others who need some more direction. Stand behind them and watch them change the world.

My children:

What are you doing now?

Son -Started working at age 15 - Universal Heating and Air, multiple certifications - Maintenance Supervisor - on call cover complex 7x24. future goal: Regional Manager multiple properties. Rent Apartment, have vehicle.

Oldest daughter - Started working at age 15 -MBA, BA degrees - elementary school teacher and bar tender – works 2 jobs - future goal: Doctorate teach at college level. Rent Apartment, have vehicle.

Youngest daughter -Started working at age 15 - BS - full time bartender and Uber eats driver – works 2 jobs future goal: MBA Counseling business. Rent house, have vehicle.

What to concentrate on in the future:

Do not settle for the position you are currently in. If you have an opportunity to advance your career and make more money do it. Don't be complacent. We all work as hard or harder than others. We deserve to be making decent money through our efforts and commitment.

Take risks. Put together a plan for your life. Look at your god given abilities. Write, draw, create, sing, rap, heal, lead, teach, etc. Use them.

Live within your means. Budget your expenses. Take care of the things you have. Make others accountable. The more money you can make the less stress/pressure you have.

Take advantage of every opportunity. Look for scholarships or grants if attending school. If your company will provide education funding use it. Network with people to gain higher paying job positions and contacts.

Save. Set up money from your paycheck to be deducted electronically to a savings account. If you don't see it you won't miss it. Even if it is $20 a paycheck it is a start. Do it now!

Never give up. We are awesome people. Smart, charming, motivated, beautiful inside and out. Don't let anyone keep you from the goals you set for yourself and family. Believe in yourself! Don't allow people to put you down. They don't count. Your effort does.

Move. Don't hold yourself back from moving to another residence/location. We moved multiple times to work to improve our living situation. The experience and education we received was priceless. We have met and know so many wonderful people through our travels.

Set goals. The only way you are going to get to where you want to be is to set goals. Daily, monthly, yearly goals will get you what you see yourself achieving. Give yourself six months to improve your situation at one hundred percent effort. Once those goals are achieved start another six months count. You will be pleasantly surprised at what gets accomplished.

Forgive Yourself

I have made plenty of mistakes in my life. Thankfully they have been learning lessons for my growth as a human being. I have done a pretty good job of forgiving those who may have hurt me. I need to do a better job of forgiving myself. Today is June 25th 2024. It is time I forgive myself and ask God for help. He understands that I have made mistakes and asked for forgiveness. Whatever setbacks I encounter from here on out are expected. I will no longer stress about them. I will laugh at them and move forward. It is time for me to become the person I was born to be. I have survived a lot and became a better person for it. I can, I will, I must endure and become stronger. That is what is expected of me.

What I Am Grateful For

My life

My health

My children

My grandchildren

My siblings

My nieces and nephews

My friends

My memories

My talents and abilities

My sense of humor

My perseverance

My faith

My food every day

My water to drink

My assistance from American River Staff

My assistance from VA staff

My assistance to be driven places

My funds to get by

My future opportunities

My chances to heal my body

My chances to stand and walk again

My chances to write stories and publish them

My chances to do PT

My chances to go outside

My opportunity to change my life and do better next time in some things

My chance to go to VA Palo Alto PT training center

My chance to move to North Dakota

Dear God,

May I have the following:

Be able to heal my wound

Be able to overcome infections

Be able to overcome kidney issues

Be able to straighten my back

Be able to stand again

Be able to move my left leg

Be able to close my left hand

Be able to walk again

Be able to write successful books

Be able to gain wealth

Be able to talk to crowds of people on stage and deliver a great message

Be able to give money to charities to help others

Be able to help veterans

Be able to spend quality time with my kids, grandkids, siblings, nieces, nephews and friends

Be able to travel to other places